SEASONS OF CHANGE

A collection of 100 poems by
KEVIN MCLACHLAN

Seasons of Change
Copyright © 2023 by Kevin McLachlan

All rights reserved. No part of this publication may be reproduced, distributed, or transmitted in any form or by any means, including photocopying, recording, or other electronic or mechanical methods, without the prior written permission of the author, except in the case of brief quotations embodied in critical reviews and certain other non-commercial uses permitted by copyright law.

Tellwell Talent
www.tellwell.ca

ISBN
978-1-998190-50-8 (Paperback)
978-1-998190-51-5 (eBook)

For: Mom, Dad, and Bryson

Table of Contents

Preface ix

SUMMER

The Garden.. 2
Nothing Has Changed.. 3
Doctor's Dilemma 4
Jon 6
1998 Mitsubishi Delica 8
Paradise.. 11
A Normal Night Doing the Laundry....................... 12
An Old Secret 14
Prayer... 16
Questions about Tomatoes 17
In the Valley of the Morning................................... 19
Thoughts of a Late-Night Snack.............................. 20
A Poem about Plums 21
The Left Side 22
Two Dear Friends.. 23
Don't Forget.. 24
Four Years Later 25
Sitting on the Floor 27
Where Does Wisdom Go 28
Old Letters... 29
Early Morning Rain 31
Tick Tock... 32

Earl Grey 34
The Heritage Rose 36
On Soft Summer Nights 38

FALL

October's Kiss 42
When the Pears Fall 44
Between the Curtains 46
For the Girl Laughing in the Waterfall 47
Alfie 48
Sweet Reunion 49
Thunder and Rain 50
What is Worth Remembering 51
In the Quiet That Remains 53
Bluebell Place 54
As I Hold You Close 55
Sick 56
Fall Wind 58
Would You Call It a Good Fight? 59
Heat 60
Falling Asleep on the Couch 61
Walking Home 62
A Murmuration 64
The Old Store on Creek Street 65
The Sweater 66
If You're Quiet 67
I Wish Not to Sleep 68
Old Flame 69
Every Old Diner 70
I Know Someone 72

WINTER

Winter	74
The Vines	75
Night Embers	77
Somewhere in Nova Scotia	78
On a December Night	79
Rain Runs Down	80
The Mural of Love	81
Gray Days	83
Hello Moon	84
One More Song	85
In Another World	87
Slow Goodbyes	88
New Friends	89
Tangled	90
Could We Pause for a Moment?	91
Fragments	92
Fireweed Drive	93
A Prayer	94
Calvin	95
I Learned a Few Things	96
Visiting Home	98
Aurora	99
I Walked Slow Today	100
People Who Come and Go	101
Crescendo	103

SPRING

Spring 106
Old Friend 107
A Good Poem 108
Courage 109
The Sunset 110
My Voice...111
Two Weeks...112
Songwriter..113
Searching for the Way 114
One Heartbeat 115
On the L 116
Happy Birthday 117
Fresh Bread 118
The Yukon 119
Learning the Piano..................................... 120
The Room in My Head............................... 122
Soft 123
The Boys on Mary Street 124
Moonbeams 125
The Stream 126
David 128
A Broken Cup Holder 129
Hush...131
Morning Light 132
Starting with Pleasure 133

About the Author...135

Preface

If you are reading this book, I would like to say thank you.

There are lots of books out there these days, and there are lots of books of poetry. This is my first published book and my first book of poems and, like all firsts, I hope there are many books that come after these and they get better as time goes on.

This book began as a challenge to write a poem every day for a year, and in this book you will find 100 of those poems, twenty-five for each season.

My hope for you, reader, is that you find a poem in here that makes you pause. A poem that makes you smile or feel warmth in your chest. A poem that makes you breathe a little slower or think a little differently or remember something special that belongs only to you.

When you have finished this book, I encourage you to give it away. Books are best when they are being read.

Thank you for taking the time to read my poetry.

—Koovy

Summer

The Garden

After thirty-three years,
My father has decided he's ready to retire.
He's tired.
And although he had the same job my whole life,
I was never quite certain
of exactly what he did.
Only that he was almost never late,
Except when I made him.
And not once did he ever complain,
Except when I made him.

The next day, I call him,
And I ask him how it feels.

Just about the same, he says.

A week later, I call him again.

What are you doing? I ask.

Weeding dandelions from my garden, he says.

And how does it feel?

Just about the same, he says.

Only it's not the same,

Because now he's in the garden.

Nothing Has Changed

My alarm still sounds the same.
I still need to get groceries
Bananas
Milk
Or I'll just pretend I don't mind almond milk
And use the rest of it up.

I water the garden
And my tomatoes grow
And turn yellow and red
While the creeping Charlie
Creeps its way in and out of the dirt
No matter how many times I pull it up

Just as you do.

Cars speed by out front
And the rabbit in my yard runs away
When I open the door.

Nothing has changed
Just us
Is now

Me
And
You

How does everyone keep pretending that nothing has changed?

When it all feels so different.

Doctor's Dilemma

Today I have to pretend I'm a doctor in a play
And I worry that I won't remember all the words,
Or where to stand
Or when to come in,

But once I've practiced my words
And my spacing
I think about this character.

A man who has chosen to take care of the less fortunate.
What a noble path, I think to myself
To pick a life of service and poverty
But to know
Every day
That you make a difference
That you save lives.

And me,
A life of pretend
A life of putting on the voice and clothes of others
And pretending it's important.

But then I think of the man
In the casino
After a performance of *We Will Rock You*,

Seasons of Change

How he stood with tears in his eyes
Thanking me,
Telling me he hadn't heard those songs in over a decade
Not since he crawled through the mud
Chasing the border
Chasing his freedom,
When all he had was an mp3
And the music of Queen.

I shook his hand.
He wiped his eyes.

At every performance
It's someone's first show
And it's someone's last
And they both deserve something good.

Jon

He's making me an omelette
And the tea is steeping
And he's grating cheese
And dicing shallots
And the pantry is full.

We didn't have plans
And he isn't even eating
Nor is his partner,
He's just making it for me
Because he thought it would be nice
And it is nice.

He tells me about his newest project
His fermented corn.
Fresh tomatoes sit on the table.
He shares a kiss with his man.

There's work in an hour
And a lot of work to be done
And maybe I should have gone home
And practiced
Or slept
Or done more research
Or eaten something lighter
Or memorized lines.
After all, it's important.

But isn't this?
This omelette
This corn

This kitchen,
Full of love as all kitchens should be.

This man,
Full of fire
And drowning in love.

Come in, he says.
The light is on.
Come eat, he says.
The food is ready.

And for an hour I am held again
By my friend
By his love
By his omelette
By his corn.

Kevin McLachlan

1998 Mitsubishi Delica

I sit,
And pretend I know anything
About my van.

I mean
Now I know a few things
Like how to change the tires
And that when the check engine light comes on
Just tighten the gas cap
Unless it's winter
Then just ignore it
And tap the accelerator and it will go away
And close the gas cap extra hard
'Cause sometimes it pops open
When you shut the side door
And don't wiggle the center console
It's loose
And could fall over
And the fog lights don't work
Never have
And the AC got fixed
But hasn't worked since
And the frame has rusted
And needs to be rebuilt near the left tire.
The little dent on the left side
Was my fault
And you can't use LED headlights
Not with the actual glass lamps
Gotta use halogen
And Matt told me not to touch the bulb
But he told me that after I put the first one in

And it smoked 'cause I touched it
And I thought I was gonna light everything on fire
And if you hold the lock button on the keys the windows will come down
Cause one time I did that
Before I knew
And came back and the windows were open
But everything was there
And the horn doesn't work
And there's a dent in the back from when I got rear-ended
So be careful when you use the back hatch
And the rear mirror is cracked too
And the front windshield in two places
One happened on the roads back home
And one from a rock in Saskatchewan.

It's not the best on gas
It's old
And beat-up
And when I bought it off that guy in Edmonton I had never even seen it
And when I picked it up from that farm
There were tires in the back

And a fork

And he should have told me the brakes needed to be replaced
And I should have bought a different van
Or just a car
But I'm glad I didn't
And I drive it almost every day
And when I got laid off and had nowhere to live
I had that van

And I lived inside
And I drove from Niagara to the Yukon
And she kept me company to whole way
And kept me safe.

I can't tell you how to change the oil
Or fix the AC
But I can tell you how it feels to wake up in the back seat lying next to the ocean
What the road feels like late at night in the middle of nowhere with the windows down
What the sunsets are like in the prairies when you're almost out of gas
What the mountains are like in the Rockies when you switch to 4WD
What that fear is like in the pit of your stomach when you wake up with nowhere to live and no one next to you
And you have to get up anyways
And sit in the back
And make oatmeal
And eat in silence.

I can't tell you how to fix the horn
Or the fog lights
But I know that van
And that van knows me
And even when I couldn't fix her
She could fix me.

Paradise

I know not what awaits
Nor the time that lasts,

But for now

This cup of tea,
Hot on my tongue

This peach,
Sweet in my mouth
Running down my hand
Like our laughter
Running through our hearts

This sun,
Warm
And warmer still
With you.

Dear friend,
If I beat you to paradise
I'll make sure I save you a seat.

Kevin McLachlan

A Normal Night Doing the Laundry

It's 2:00 a.m.
Socks in the top drawer
T-shirts folded
Then rolled
I have too many
But I like getting new ones.

Pants
Bottom drawer
Also rolled
I have several
And more green ones than I realized.

Another t-shirt
This one is full of holes
But I can't bring myself to throw it out.

I remember this shirt falling into my hands
In the thrift shop in Victoria
Living in my van
Fresh tea and fresh rain
Homeless
Aimless
Rhythm it reads on the breast pocket
I wore it almost every day
Waking up in the back of my van
On the shores
Of French Beach
Or by the Sooke Potholes
Stretching it over my body
As I lit the fire

And cooked breakfast

Alone

Silent

But the whispers of the wood.

I'll wear it again tomorrow
And David will comment on all the holes
And tell me to throw it away
I'll smile and say that I will soon.

He's in the hall laughing at my shirt

I'm at the ocean

Listening to the rhythm of the waves.

Kevin McLachlan

An Old Secret

The first time I was in love
We were together for two years.

We moved around a lot
Living together
And apart
And a part of each other.

In the morning
I'd usually be the first one out,
And awake or asleep
I'd kiss her goodbye
Then as I left the room
I'd stop,
Halfway out the door
Rush back in
And kiss her
One more time.

I didn't think of it as something
Special
It was just
A nice thing to do
And loving her
Was nice.

She fell in love
With someone else
So she left.

Seasons of Change

And while many have come and gone since
I don't stop in the doorway anymore
I just go.

I still save that
Not for her
Or for me
But for us
What we shared
What we held

What we lost.

Prayer

I find myself awake
In the throes of midnights
Asking
Can I mend the seams I've torn?

I have hurt
A hurt beyond my repair
And my hands and my heart
Seem not strong enough
To save it.

Given half a breath
I would do anything asked of me
So I strain to listen
In the quiet of the moonlight.

A voice murmurs back
Then leave me be
And I wish
For something else.

Questions about Tomatoes

Does a tomato know
How to grow?
How red
Or yellow
Or orange
To turn?

Does it settle in the sun
And think
Ah yes, just this
Or does it
Wiggle in the dark
And sigh
With the moon
And the crickets
And the weeds.

Is it proud
Of the beautiful fruit
It becomes?
Juicy
Sweet
And
Fresh.

Does it hurt
to be plucked from the vine?

How does it know
When there's nowhere left to go?
Or grow?

Oh.

How do any of us know?

In the Valley of the Morning

Do the roses
At my window
Dream to fly
As I do?

Or

Have they learned
To be content
With their thorns?

Kevin McLachlan

Thoughts of a Late-Night Snack

It's 1:00 am
I'm eating the last piece of carrot cake.
It's very good.
Maybe a little old,
Not stale
But getting there.

Silly idea really
Carrots in cake,
But it is quite delicious.

I wonder who thought of it first:
Let's add carrots.
A visionary?
A fool?

What's next
Broccoli pudding?
Probably not.

Let's leave the visions
For the visionaries
And the dreams
For the dreamers

And the cake
For me.

After all,
It's very good.

A Poem about Plums

It must be tough
Being a plum,
The forgotten fruit.
Never making it to kindergarten classes for the letter "P"
Always losing out to
Pony
Or
Pickle
Or
Penny
Or
Maybe not 'penny' anymore.
I suppose I'm getting older.
Poor Plum,
Never making it to the juice aisle,
Or as a spread,
Rarely appearing on grocery lists
Or in trees requested
And yet
Somehow
Every time I see a plum
I'm reminded,
Oh yeah,
Plums.
Not bad,
Not bad at all.

The Left Side

What does it mean
To wake up
Without you?

I had gotten so used to your face
Greeting mine
That once it left
I still looked for its outline
Its shadow on the pillow.

Funny,
How nothing
Feels more empty
Than what was.

I haven't touched
The left side of my bed
In months.

Two Dear Friends

Two hearts
Laughing
Crying
One with wine
The other
With tea.

Lamenting
Over lovers lost.

We ask each other,
When does it go away?
When do we stop loving?

But we both know
We won't stop,
And we don't want to

Not while there's still tea,
And wine,
And friendship.

Don't Forget

When you find yourself behind the wheel
Leaving again,

To ask yourself,

Going towards?
Or
Running from?

It's all the same road.

Four Years Later

Tonight,
All of a sudden
Here you are.
And we talk,
Not as if we're old friends,
We're not anymore.
But as if
We're both too polite to acknowledge
That is has been a long time.

I say *hello*.
And you say *hi*.
You were great in the show.
Really you were.
You say *thanks*,
And I give you a hug.

Did you hold on,
Just a little longer?

Or did I imagine that.

I swear for one second.
I forgave those four years.
Just holding you.
Feeling you hold me,

Did you hold on,
Just a little longer?

Did I hold on,
After all these years?

Not like it matters,
We never were a great fit.

But,
We tried.
We fit as best we could.
Not every puzzle has to be perfect
To be worthwhile.

I guess
It doesn't matter
Even if you did.
Maybe you will again,
In four more years.

You were amazing tonight.
Really you were.

Did you hold on,
Just a little longer?

Have I been holding on,
All this time?

Sitting on the Floor

All these chairs
And yet
We find ourselves
Sitting on the floor
With pizza
And paper napkins.

It's not half as comfortable,
But I like it more.

Us
The floor
The pepperoni.

So this is falling in love?

Even easier
Than I thought.

Kevin McLachlan

Where Does Wisdom Go

Where does wisdom go
When it finally slips from lips?
Does it drift until it bumps into someone
Or must it be picked up and cared for?

What about love?
When it doesn't make its way back,
A fisherman casting his net in the water.
Is it really so bad to catch only the sea?

And what of laughter?
Once it's filled our cheeks and hearts,
Who gets to keep it?
Or are the memories enough?
After all,
They take so long to make.

Lastly, what of grief?
Who comes to the table uninvited,
But stays so long as we save him a seat.
How long must we sit with the shadow of ourselves
Before we turn off the light?

And what of now?
Silent.
Sipping tea.
How will I know when it's over,
If no one tells me it's begun.

Old Letters

Today,
I was going through old boxes
Old books
Giving things away
Throwing things out
And I came across your letter:
Open when you miss me.

I read it
And I missed you.

For a moment I was on that ferry
Smelling the sea,
Feeling the cool ocean breeze,
And hearing your crocs on the deck,
Your little laugh,
"*Hey, kid.*"

Then I found the rest of them:

Open when you're mad at me

Open when you're sad

Open when you're happy

Open when you've had a bad day

I can't bring myself to do it,
To open any more,
So I put them all away
Back in a book
On my shelf.

I must be missing one:

Open when you've lost me.

Early Morning Rain

When was the last time
You went out
And stood
In the rain
Looked up
At the heavens
And let the water
Run down your face
Like the sky
Was crying for you?

Have you forgotten
That you used to love the rain?

Come, my friend
Hear it falling,
Calling.

Remember
How glorious it is
To be alive.

Tick Tock

I have always
Hated clocks
That tick loudly.

A metronome
To time
Beating past
In its
Consistent meter.

Filling the silence
With a begrudging
March
Of tick and tock
Over and over.

Silence
Would be simpler.

I promise
Time will still
Move past,

And if you still
Feel the need
To hear something
That reminds you
Of the moments
Slipping by

Seasons of Change

Listen
To your heart beat.
Your breath rise
And fall.

You too
Are keeping time.

Earl Grey

The kettle
Yells from the stovetop
And I run to the kitchen
As if I should be surprised
That it's calling
When I was the one
Who put it there.

I could get an electric one
But I always forget
To go check if it's boiled
So I leave a tea bag
In a mug
Dry
Next to a kettle of boiled water
Abandoned.

I have more mugs
Than a person would ever need
And I run my hands
Along the stories of each one
Like the potter's hands
Before me.
I scoop the tea leaves in
P
 O
  U
 R
And watch as the water
Whirls them around,
A torrent

Of heat and memory
And the smell
Of Bergamot and Assam
Dances up
On the steam.

I could not tell you
Exactly what this tea tastes like
It's just leaves and water

But
If you have ever sat in the garden
And watched the roses
Push up to the heavens
And the tomatoes redden on the vine
Or seen the way the squirrel listens
Or the rabbit pauses
And you have thought to yourself
As the sun warmed you
It is good
To be alive

Then I need not tell you,
You already know.

The Heritage Rose

For so long
I thought of myself as the rose,
Grown from the bush
Prickled and rough
Bursting out
In a flare
Of colour
And beauty.

Emerging to the heavens
In a display
Of vitality
And life
And love
And lust
Red
Or
Pink
As if to say
Here I am
Only to fade
And fall
And wither away.

It is only now
That I consider
Maybe I am the bush.

Seasons of Change

Incredibly ordinary
And simple
And strong
Patient
Slow.

For as the petals fall
The roots crawl
Persistent
And
Patient
Growing
Day by day.

On Soft Summer Nights

Sometimes
I just go sit by the park
At night
In my car.

If it's warm
I'll get out
And sit on a swing

Something
About the quiet
The moment alone

Grounds
Me
Lands
Me

I guess
I just miss being a kid
And playing
In the park.

That just seems
Simpler

I hear you

Calling

Laughing

Seasons of Change

Sun shining
On the swing
I shout out
Even now

Higher

Higher

Fall

October's Kiss

Has just landed
Soft and sweet
Cool and crisp.

The sun
Is growing tired
And wakes slow
And lies early.

Even the leaves
Can't find the strength
To hold on any longer
And after a summer
Of green

They turn.

A kaleidoscope
Of colour and shape
As they carpet the path
Outside my house
And decorate the water
With leafy kisses.

The birds
Are a little busier

The squirrels a bit
Squirrellier.

Seasons of Change

October's kiss
Has come.
Whether it's welcome or not
Has come.

As it always does
And always will

Long after me
Long after you

Just as change
Always will.

When the Pears Fall

There is a pear tree in my yard.
Well,
Actually three
And in the spring they grow
Beautiful white flowers
And then all summer long
They slowly grow their fruit
Until fall arrives
And the fruit too
Begin to fall.

The backyard fills with rabbits
And squirrels
And my friends,
Anyone who wants a pear.

I'm told if I thin the fruit earlier
The pears will grow bigger,

But I never do

The tree doesn't seem to mind.

I'm told
A single pear tree can't grow fruit
They have to grow alongside another
That's why they call them pears,
And I've never checked if that's true.

Seasons of Change

I liked it too much
To chase if it's true.

What's more beautiful,
The blossom
The fruit
Or
The growing together?

Do the single 'pair' trees
Know they are missing fruit?

Do they still blossom?

They're still a pear tree
Even when alone
Even when no fruit falls.

Between the Curtains

A smile,
A laugh,
And an ocean.

A glimpse,
Into the truth
Of a moment,
Of simplicity.

Until the water runs cold.

She laughs,
And I know
This laughter
Runs warm
And runs deep.

My heart,
Which has run cold
For some time now,
Sparks.

Somewhere,
Between the curtains,
Lies my heart.

For the Girl Laughing in the Waterfall

I think
I could wait forever
For you.

I think
I'd rather
Not wait
Another second.

Alfie

Young blood,
It's good to see you, brother
Been a minute, eh?
You look good,
You crazy cat.
How you been?

We hug.

Yo, no man, you heard about this? Try this.

We switch sides of the hug.

Heart to heart, bro, heart to heart.

These are the words
Of a great friend,
Of a great man,
I would do anything for.

Sweet Reunion

Somewhere
Before now
We knew each other.

In another life
Or this one.

Before this night
This kiss
This embrace.
You,
Outlining my chin
With your hands,
My heart
With your laugh,

Somewhere
These souls
Had met.

Thunder and Rain

I read a story about a man
Who died chasing a storm

I shook my head
And called him a fool

Then I called you.

What is Worth Remembering

I could not tell you
What I had for breakfast yesterday
Or even
What day of the week it is.

I'm not one of those people
Who can remember the date of
A concert
Or a wedding
Or a show.

In fact
Sometimes I worry
At how often I forget.

Birthdays
Are especially bad
I always get them just
A bit mixed up.

But here
As you fall asleep
Head tucked in the pillow
Fan blowing
Because you need white noise
Blanket tucked to your chest
I don't think
I've ever forgotten a kiss

Or a goodnight
Or what your lips first felt like
Or the first time I heard you laugh

Yes,
Especially your laugh.

In the Quiet That Remains

My house feels vacant
In the absence of you.

Sullen in silence
Alone anew.

Bluebell Place

Most days
I check the weather back home.
I like to know what kinda day it's gonna be
And how Mom and Dad are.

It's warm here today,
Thirteen degrees and it's the end of October
But cold back home
Minus three and snowing
And tomorrow the low is minus nine.

Whenever people ask about the Yukon
I always joke that at least it's warm here in Ontario
And they say something like
Yeah, I could never live there
Or
Why would anyone want to live somewhere so cold?
And I laugh and shrug.

But if you spend one day up there

In January
With the cold prying the air out of your lungs
And the snow coming down sweetly
The trees hugged with the hoarfrost
The ice clinging to your eyelashes
In a world so untamed
They say God was tired when he made it

Then you would not ask such questions.

As I Hold You Close

You feel strong, soft, and safe
You smell of poetry, peonies, and patience
You taste of sunshine, summer, and secrets.

Sick

There are days
Where I feel like a man
Strong and gentle
And days
Where I feel
Independent
And grown.

I wake in the house I rent.
Tend the garden I grow.
I go to the job I do
And I do it well.

I clean the house
Or tidy the yard.
I call a friend
Or go to the gym.

But I am always reminded
Of where I came from
And who I am
When I awake to find
That I am sick.

And while I now know how
To take care of myself,

What I want to do
More than anything
Is to stay in bed
And to call out

Mom

And to feel her hand
Cool on my brow.

Fall Wind

Come
Blow away
This sadness
That sits on my heart.

Lift me
Like you do the mounds of leaves

And float me away
To heaven's gate
Or the open ocean.

Where do you go sweet wind
When no one is watching
When you no longer toss and turn?

Do you wish to just be still?

Would You Call It a Good Fight?

The effort we put in
To loving each other.

Did we fight
Tooth and nail
For this thing
No one else believed in?

I guess they were right
'Cause here we are
Bell rung
And no words exchanged.

I suppose it's what we get
For calling it a fight
But god
What a good
Good fight
Learning how to love
The way you love.

We didn't win
But we sure didn't lose
Right or wrong
That's true.

Heat

You did not know
And so I am not angry

But you should know

That when your fire inside
Grew so big it had to burn off
And you turned those flames on me

While I never raised my voice
Or burned back
I held those embers
In my cracked hands
And watched them extinguish my flames

So while I did not burn back
I burned within
Until you didn't understand
Why I had no heat left for you

Falling Asleep on the Couch

Now when I fall asleep on the couch
No one carries me to bed.

When I wake up
I'm still on the couch,
I still live alone,
I still miss my dad.

I can't remember the last time
He carried me to bed
In his tired gentle hands

And I doubt either of us knew
That it would be the last.

Kevin McLachlan

Walking Home

This morning
It was cold and crisp,
But the sun shone
And the cars flew by.

I passed the swamp,
The water murky and green
The surface glassy and still.

I took a moment
To look upon it,

And saw

My reflection
Staring back at me.

I almost didn't recognize
The man looking back,
Hair long and unkempt
Grays sneaking in the sides,
Lines in the forehead.

But a glint
In the eyes.

Seasons of Change

Full of spark
And flame
For the world around.

For the first time in years
I saw myself.

A Murmuration

Above, a murmuration
Beautiful,
I whisper.

Isn't it incredible
The way the birds
All move together,
Like a wave
Rippling
Coursing
Tugging at the corners
Of the sky.

And then,
Three of them
At the exact same time,

Shit directly on my windshield.

I mean
They're just birds.

The Old Store on Creek Street

As I wander
The antique store
I wonder
If anything I own
Will ever end up here.

Oh, wow.
They might say.
Look at that hand carved spoon.

Or

Look at that old teapot, I had one just like that.

And then walk past it
As it collects dust.

At least that's doing something, collecting dust.

I'll be dead.

So someone might as well have a nice cup of tea.

The Sweater

When I woke today
I heard that someone had died
And then
I worried about what sweater to wear
To breakfast.

If You're Quiet

You can hear two people laughing
And whispering
Up in the balcony
In the very last row.
They both left a party
That just started.

And if you listen real close
You can hear the creaks of the building
The rush of the wind outside
The hum of the ghost light
The whisper
Of two hearts
Talking
And being heard.

I Wish Not to Sleep

Sleep leads me to you.
The sweetness of the dreams
Like honey
Melting into my spirit.

Then the morning,

Leads me back
To the quiet

Like frost
Creeping in
With the softness of the night.

Old Flame

A moment
In the grocery store
Where a stranger passes.
The scent
Of a shadow
Of someone
I remember.

Suddenly
I am brought back
To your room
To your laugh
And to
My first hard goodbye
And our first true love.

Or so we thought.

And then
They walk past
And I go back
To picking apples.

It is nice to think of you
After all these years.

Thank you for the gentle way
In which you taught me of love
In which you taught me
How little I knew.

Every Old Diner

I love diners
The way
They all feel the same.

The potatoes change
Home fries here
Deep fried down the street
Crispy bacon up north
Chewy in the city.

They all smell like grease.

I drink out of a plastic cup
And ask for more water for my tea.

Over-easy eggs
All taste the same.

An older woman
Calls me sweetie
Or dear
Or hon
And I tip well
As if I have the money to do it.
I eat cheap toast
And I put ketchup on my potatoes.

Seasons of Change

I watch the gray
In my hair grow longer
My days
Grow shorter
And I sit in the booth
Just a little longer
Than I should.

Kevin McLachlan

I Know Someone

Who loves gently
Like fog.
Slowly and sweetly
With tender hands
And simple words.

It is hard
To trust this love
When you've only known
Smoke.
It seems the same
the smoke
Until it stings your eyes
And burns your lungs
And you can't breathe.

But the fog
While sometimes cold
Wraps you up
And holds you tenderly.
It is safe here
In the folds
Of this love.

Winter

Winter

The night comes
Sooner and sooner
As winter creeps in.

Even the sun
Is tired
Of getting up so early,

And the chill
Of November
Seeps in
Through the cracks
Of night.

It is awful cold
And dark
And quiet
And harsh

And yet
There is a beauty
In the chill
In the ice
In the night.

The Vines

It's cool this morning
And as I step out to greet the day
It hits me
The smell of smoke.

I smile
With memories
Of campfires
Come
And
Gone
And the laughter that comes with it.

That smell always takes me back
To crawling into my tent
Heart full
Belly full
And eyes aglow
With laughter
And love.

The grapes
Have come
And gone
The wine has been made
And in preparation for next season
The burning begins.

Sweet is the smoke
With its years of wine.

Drink up
For winter
Has come.

Night Embers

I sit by the fire
Surrounded by friends

We drink
And laugh
And carve sticks
To roast marshmallows,

The shadows of the flames
Dance on our smiling faces
Marshmallows stick to our fingers
And the embers glow bright.

The evening never ends.

And I am awake in a dream.

Kevin McLachlan

Somewhere in Nova Scotia

A man
Whom I have never met
And who I am told
Is my grandfather
Died this year.

It's a little confusing
Not knowing
If I should feel sad or not.

I cannot speak to him
Or of him,

But today I learned
That he wrote many cards to his wife
And never missed a chance to say he loved her
And she kept every single one
He ever gave her
In their 59 years together.

May time and love
Move through me
In the way they moved through him.

On a December Night

I just left the bar
With a beautiful woman
And she holds my arm.

We don't say a word
We just walk
And breathe.

And I wish for a moment
That the walk to the car

Took forever.

Rain Runs Down

I'm sitting in the passenger seat
Staring out the window
Watching raindrops
Race down the pane
Trying to guess which one
Will reach the bottom first.

I didn't think I'd be on this drive
So soon.
I didn't think I'd be in the passenger seat.
I didn't think I'd think of you
The way I do.

I guess I went and fell in love.
I hope you did too.

It's not the same though.
It's never the same.

The Mural of Love

This morning
I sat and drank tea
With a friend
I have known for many years.

Every love is special
She reminds me
But no love is ever the same.

Look at the painting of life,

As some enter
The painting shifts,
Mountains are added
Trees are placed
And as some go
The mountains fade
The trees thin
Or we find ourselves
Somewhere else entirely.

When you arrived
It wasn't just mountains or trees
It was color.

All my life
I'd been painting in gray
But you were crimson red and skyfall blue.

Eventually, you left.

But everything
Is still streaked
With red and blue.

Gray Days

It is easier to write
On gray days
And rainy mornings
When the world is too quiet and cold
To hum with life.

I find myself drinking from the same mug,
Holding the same pen,
Staring at the same empty pages,
Waiting for the rain
To spring to life my words
As it does the flowers.

I wait.

And wait.

Like the old men
Who sit on their balconies
Watching the world
Rush past.
What are they waiting for?

Hello Moon

Hello moon
It's day
You should be resting
For the sun is up
And out
And bright
And brilliant.

But secretly
I am very
Very
Happy to see you.

One More Song

It is a funny thing
Knowing that our time is running out
Knowing that this slow dance
In your living room
By the fire
In the gentle hours of the morning
With the candles
And the flowers
Might be our last.

Does it make it more special
Knowing that it must happen now?
For it won't happen at our wedding
Or on Sunday mornings
While we make breakfast.

Perhaps it just makes it harder
Feeling it slip out of our grasp
Knowing that no song is long enough
And that eventually we must let it go.

Just as winter
Will always turn to spring,
Time slips away
Just like you.

But still
We dance
As your cheek rests on mine
And the song plays out.

Oh my love,
I don't want you to go
Not just yet
Stay with me
For one more song.

In Another World

I wake up next to you today.
I watch your chest rise and fall
Admire the tapestry of your sleep.

We walk home
And we laugh
And it takes much longer than it should
Because it's nice not to rush
With someone like you.

We dance in the kitchen
And lie on the couch
And trade heartbeats

But that is all in another world.

Instead
We part.

And in days
Or weeks
Or months
Or years
From now

When someone speaks of you,

Ask the moon,
I will say
Ask what it has seen.

Kevin McLachlan

Slow Goodbyes

Here is a cheers
To the slow exits
And the dragged departures.

The farewells that begin in the kitchen
Then dip into the foyer
That linger on the front step
Then drag into the driveway.

I once knew a lover
That rushed out
Always on time
Always direct
Quick into the car
And home right away
With time to spare.

To spare for what?
For whom?

Of all the time I have to spend
I'd like to spend most of it on the front step
Hugging one more time
Cracking one last joke
And taking one more moment
To go slow.

New Friends

I am making friends
With the birds and the leaves.

Getting to know the wind
And the spring.

I've heard them for years
But I am only getting acquainted now.

They don't seem to mind
That it's taken me this long
To ask how they are
And how they've been.

When I stop
And listen
They tell me.

Tangled

I am tangled
On the floor of the hallway
In cinnamon and vanilla
And sorrow and longing.

It drips off of me
And in to you
As I taste your sweetness
And the ache of us.

Could We Pause for a Moment?

I'd like just a moment to imagine
The ocean,
And not you standing in front of me
Ankle deep in the water.

To imagine
The rain,
And not you laughing underneath it
Next to me.

To imagine
Sleep,
And not the rise and fall of your chest
Against my body.

To imagine
Nothing,
And not still somehow
Wish it was with you.

Fragments

If I called
Would you pick up?

Could we pick up
Where we left off?

A heart breaks
Like a pane of glass

And no one
Can ever clean
All of it up

Fireweed Drive

I walk next door
Through the cold.
The stars reflecting off the snow,
And the ice lanterns
Guide me down the driveway.
The fire roars outside
And the hockey sticks lie next to the pond.

Two dogs I've never seen greet me,
And I hug my friends
Some of whom I haven't seen in years
Some of whom I haven't seen in hours.

We laugh,
The house hums
With music
And laughter
And the sound of crokinole.

This is how it feels to be home.

A Prayer

May you be loved
In the way you deserve
Unbounded and undefeated.

May you arrive
At the meadows
Of your dreams.

Calvin

A new year
So I sit with an old friend
We drink tea
And talk about our dreams.

He is grown now
And owns a house
And has a woman he loves very much.

Little has changed from yesterday
To today,

But from years past
To now,

It seems little has stayed the same.

How nice to have an old friend.
How nice to have a new year.

May they keep
Side by side
With each one to come.

Kevin McLachlan

I Learned a Few Things

I learned a few things
This past year,
Or at least was taught a few.
The learning takes a little longer.

One friend taught me to go slow
And to be patient.

And another
How to hold a heart
And not break it.
(That one takes lots of practice.)

Time taught me
I'm not in charge of anything.

And the weather
Showed me
I must wear layers
And I must be grateful.

The fox
Down the street
Showed me how to look cool
Even when eating garbage.

And the Christmas tree
Taught me
Everyone should dress up
Even just once in a while.

Seasons of Change

The sunrise
Taught me
Getting up early
Can be good.

And the moonrise
Taught me
Pay attention
To things that are special.
Most things are.

It is nice
To learn
How little you know.

Visiting Home

Strange when home becomes a parking spot,
Telling everyone what you're doing with your life
Over cups of coffee
Bragging or apologizing
Depending on the day.

A handful of stops
At favourite spots.
Try the new ones
Complain about something that's changed.

And then leave
And do it again next year.

You want to say it's still your place
But eventually
The new floors
And fresh paint
All add up to something.

You just recognize the building

And don't know who lives in it.

Aurora

Northern Lights
Danced tonight in the sky
A river
Of green and pink
Splashing and curling
Weaving a tapestry
High above
And way across.

On a canvas
Bigger than I will ever know.

I Walked Slow Today

I walked slow today
Down your old street
Glancing at every face
Hoping one of them would be yours
Not even noticing
That I'd landed at your door.

I stood for a moment
Just out front,

I could see the stairs through the glass
And hear music,

Then I kept walking

And I didn't look back.

People Who Come and Go

It didn't hit me
Until I got off the train
Standing at the top of the stairs
This was the last place I saw you.

We stood on that staircase
And kissed
And I told you I loved you
And you told me you loved me
And then I left.
Less than 24 hours in your city
Then I flew home.

There's millions of people who live here,
And you don't even live in the same neighborhood anymore.

But standing here
I'm convinced
For a moment
That the next face around the corner
Is going to be yours.

That you'll glance up
And see me
As if I've been waiting for you
All this time.

So I wait,
Longer than I should
As people come and go
And you aren't one of them.

This is my life now,
Full of people
Who come and go

And you aren't one of them.

Crescendo

It rains here
The same way I fell in love with you.

Not slowly
With a growing crescendo

But sudden
And all at once

A great storm
Bursting forth
Saying
There is only
Now.

Spring

Spring

Strange
The way things change.

The seasons
The time.

They change slowly
Patiently
With ease
Such grace
That I can barely notice
Until suddenly,

It's spring.

We too have changed
Like the fruit on the vine
We have ripened
Slowly
But together.

Old Friend

I'm on a ship
Out to sea
I look
And I listen

Just the gulls
And the waves
And the echo
Of your laughter.

When I look past the shore
I see a shadow
That I know
Is only light

But for a moment
I let it be you

Sailing home
Back home
To me.

A Good Poem

A good poem
Is like fresh bedsheets
My friend Bec says
Sunburnt
And anxious
But smiling
And laughing.

I know what she means
And I can't quite explain it
But she's right
They feel the same
The poem and the bedsheets
Like a gentle wave
Or a tender hand
They both know
How to hold something softly.

I have said goodbye
So many times
I thought I had gotten good at it.

I am not good at it
Just good at pretending
That it's easy.

Courage

Let us sit
Quiet
While music plays
And strangers pass
And listen.

The wind down the street
Blows a tune of time
And the cobblestones
Echo out a drumbeat
With drunken footsteps.

Let us make music
And art
And poetry
And prose.

Instead
We walk home alone
Wishing we had the courage.

The Sunset

I have missed hundreds of sunsets
Were they all as beautiful as this?
This warm,
This soft.

What else have I missed?

Who else
Have I watched slip away
Slowly and gently?

My Voice

I am losing my voice,
Mostly from singing too loud
And not enough water
And certainly
Not enough sleep.

Not the way I lost it with you.

By sealing it away
And trading it in for shrugs
And nods
To make things
Easier.

But that wasn't easier
For anybody.

Two Weeks

It has been two weeks now
Met with only silence.

I wish for you everywhere.
On every bus
On every train

I don't listen to music
Or read
I look up and around

Your name on my lips
Hoping that I find you.
Terrified that I will.

Songwriter

I pick up the guitar
And my fingers wander
Searching for a melody.

At times
The music
Has become a place
To put the hurt and the heart

It holds it gently.

Tonight these six strings
Offer no solutions,

Just a backdrop
To a broken heart.

Searching for the Way

I pick up this old guitar
And ask it for words
But it just stares back
Nothing to say.

One Heartbeat

If I close my eyes
I can feel your head on my chest.

My heart slows
As does my breath
To match yours.

We sink

We sync

One heartbeat
In two chests.

On the L

I like to close my eyes
On the train.

I imagine you in the seat across from me
Reading
Or asleep
And I see the sunlight on your skin
Reflecting off your glasses.

I check my ticket
To see what time we arrive
But I can't quite make it out
I can't see what city we left
Or in what town we will stop.

Happy Birthday

Another day older
Probably a bit wiser
But still not that wise.

A bit more tired perhaps
But not too tired.

A few less friends
But a few more
Who are friends I want around.

This is getting old.

A bit scarier every year
But I like
Who I am walking beside.

Fresh Bread

Sometime just before midnight
A man arrives at my door
Hands steaming
Holding a piping hot loaf of fresh bread
Rosemary and cheddar.

Just thought
You might like this
He tells me.

I thank him
And he leaves.

Soon after I find myself
With a smile on my face
Eating over the sink.

I have very wonderful friends.

The Yukon

Wild,
Like that feeling in your heart
When waves
Crash into the shore.

Wild,
Like the pounding in your chest
When you chase after love
Knowing it could break you.

Wild,
For only when life
Appearing in trees
And animals
And abundance
Is overwhelming
And all around
And only when death
Is one wrong turn in the bush
One night in the cold
One animal in the wood

Only when life and death
Are here at your doorstep
Close enough to kiss
Do you understand
Your place in the meaning of things.

Kevin McLachlan

Learning the Piano

Do you remember that scene in *Groundhog Day*
When Bill Murray goes and takes piano lessons?

And at the end of the movie
He sits down, plays, and is incredible.

I'd do that too
If I woke up and had to live the same day every day.
I'd go learn piano.
And the cello.
I've always liked the way they sound
Rich and soft and low.

I'd learn Spanish
And take walks.
I'd get to know the animals
And maybe myself.

I'd learn how to make a good cup of coffee.
How to meditate.
I'd memorize where the sun hits the snow
And how the wind feels on my skin.
I'd watch the grass push up towards the sun
And listen to the trees stretching their roots
Down and out.

Seasons of Change

I wonder if I would be lonely
The only one repeating every day
Or if I would grow tired
Of the repetition.

I wonder
If I'd still think about you.

Kevin McLachlan

The Room in My Head

Today
I painted my room blue.

The room in my head
Where I go to be alone.

For so long
It has been whitewashed walls
That are cracked
And peeling
And no art on the walls.

Now
They are cracked
And peeling
And no art on the walls
But blue.

Maybe tomorrow
I'll paint it green.

Maybe next week
I'll fix the cracks.

Soft

Soft,
Is the sun
The way it kisses the morning,

Sweet,
Is the grass
The way it stretches in the dirt,

Sharp,
Is the breeze
The way it rushes down the trail.

Serene,
Is the tulip
The way it presses to the sky.

Shy,
Is the heart
The way it yearns for more.

Kevin McLachlan

The Boys on Mary Street

There is mud on the floor
Several noodles as well.

Boots are everywhere
And of all the toys
The item being played with
Is a cardboard box
That used to hold Eggos.

It is being thrown into the air
And caught on each kid's head
Which will surely result in tears.

These three little boys
Know so little
And I teach them today about
Howling monkeys
And why wooden spoons are hard
But sticks aren't.

They teach me
About playing in the sun
About how interesting mud is
About how hard basketball is
About how delicious Mr. Noodles are
Provided you have an ice cube.

They teach me
About the whole universe
And how you can find it all
In a cardboard box.

Moonbeams

Take the moonlight
Pull it down
And around.

Wrap me
With your cool shade
And gentle hues.

Let us drift
On moonbeams.

Kevin McLachlan

The Stream

This morning
I take care of the boy
From down the street.

His parents are busy
And need an hour of respite
So we walk
Then play by the stream.

He is little
And says only yes or no.

We race sticks
Under the bridge
We throw rocks
And listen to them splash
We even share a granola bar.

There is nothing easy
About looking after a two-year-old.

But it is simple.

There is only the present
The rocks
The sticks
The stream.

All infinitely interesting
All important
All worth at the very least
An hour
On a sunny morning
In May.

David

I have a friend
A good friend
Who I love
Who every time he visits
We make pancakes
And we drink tea
We cook thick-cut bacon
If we can afford it
We fry eggs
And we laugh
And we dance.

He tells me about his travels
And his lives
His loves
And I tell him of mine.

We hug
We part
And days
Weeks
Even months go by.

But time means nothing
To friendship.
To pancakes.

A Broken Cup Holder

My hands were full today
Taking everything out of the car.

Groceries
My bag
An empty can.

As I pull it from the van
I'm reminded of the day you
Accidentally broke the cup holder
Putting in a thermos too fast
Or maybe it was too heavy
Or maybe it was just old
And it snapped in the cold weather.

I was so upset.
Fixing it was expensive
And I hadn't had the car very long.

Now,
I wonder why I was even mad.

I haven't seen you in two years now.

I would turn back time
Just to watch you break it again.

Kevin McLachlan

I would smile
And say it's okay
And ask if you don't mind
Holding the thermos.

Then we would drive
Quietly together
Until the roads run out.

Hush

Hush
Says the night
Sleep softly in the cold.

Summer leans in
But spring
Has yet to part.
They dance

The daytime
Belongs to summer
And the night
Belongs to spring.

We walk between both
Sweetly embracing
It all.

Morning Light

Something in the morning light
Always feels softest.
Day breaks
And for a moment
We can begin again.

Starting with Pleasure

I am learning,
How to start with pleasure
As Paulus has asked me to do.
Examining the joy in my life
And then sitting with it at the wheel
Shaping my future with my own hands

I am learning,
How to be courageous
As Paulus has asked me to do.
And make something out of my pain,
Whittling away at the edges
Sanding down the sides.

I am learning,
I hope,
The difference between
Making a living
And
Making a life.

About the Author

Kevin 'Koovy' McLachlan is an author, actor, dancer, singer/songwriter from Whitehorse, Yukon. This is his first published book. Kevin has also written an original play entitled *Fragments* which was presented as part of the Paprika Festival at Native Earth Theatre in Toronto, Ontario. Koovy is the book and lyricist for *Klondike the Musical*, a Canadian musical written alongside his writing partner and friend Calvin Laveck. Koovy has also written and recorded four original albums. *Small Town* and *Moments* are under his full name Kevin McLachlan and *The Promise* and *Coming in to Peace* are under his nickname Koovy. All four albums are available on all streaming platforms. At the time of publishing, Koovy is performing in his fifth season at the Shaw Festival in Niagara-on-the-Lake, Ontario, where he is performing a brand new original show he created entitled *The Troubadour*. If you'd like to stay in touch, he is on instagram @koovster and can be contacted through his website *www.koovy.ca*.

www.ingramcontent.com/pod-product-compliance
Lightning Source LLC
LaVergne TN
LVHW040102080526
838202LV00045B/3741